YOUNG PEOPLE OF THE BIBLE

The BIG Brother

Text by BETTY SMITH
Art by NORM HAMDORF

LUTTERWORTH PRESS
GUILDFORD AND LONDON

First British Edition 1980
Copyright © 1978 Lutheran Publishing House, Adelaide.
Printed in Hong Kong

Once in the land of Canaan, there lived a very large family. Most of the sons were married with wives and children of their own. Their family tents were grouped around the big one of

their father Jacob, so that it was like a
little township. In the big tent, the two
youngest sons lived with their father.
Joseph was in his teens and Benjamin a
little boy of five.

It should have been a happy place, but it was just the opposite. The trouble was that Jacob loved Joseph more than all the rest, and said so openly. This was not only unkind, but stupid and it was Jacob's fault that all the trouble happened.

He gave Joseph a new
coat. It had long
sleeves and reached almost
to the ground. It was
made of finest wool
in several colours.
Naturally, Joseph was
very proud of it
and wore it
whenever he
could.

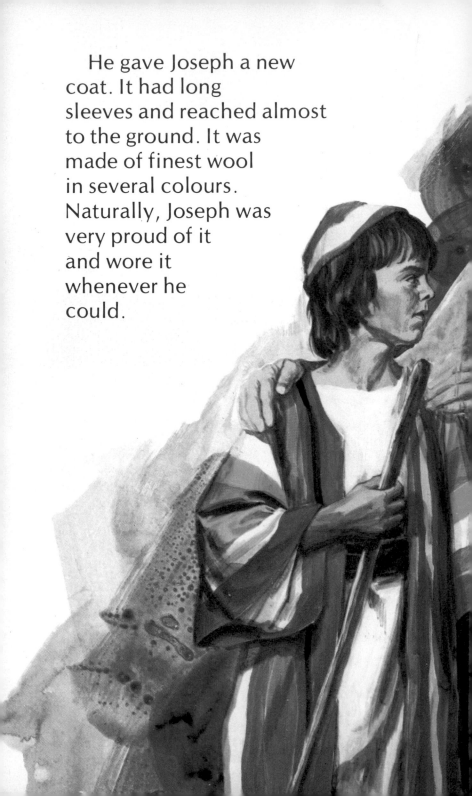

It seems a
silly thing for
grown men
to make a
fuss about, but
the brothers
were furious.
They had always
disliked their young
brother — now
they hated him.

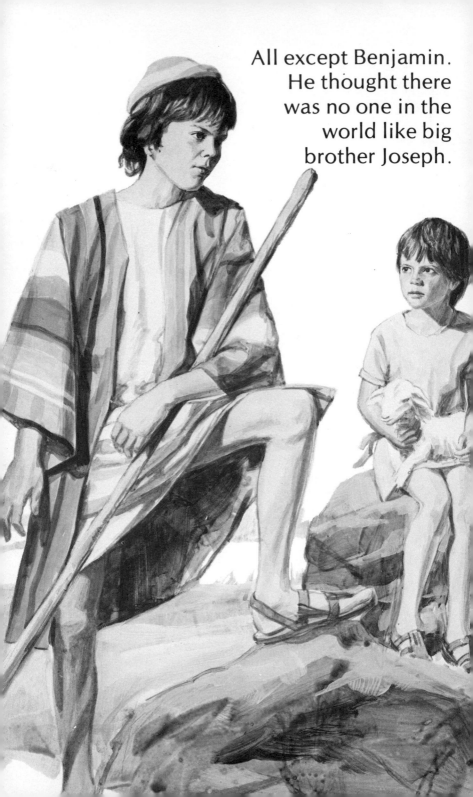

All except Benjamin.
He thought there
was no one in the
world like big
brother Joseph.

And Joseph loved and looked after his little brother. He often talked to him.

"Why do the others hate you, Joseph?" Benjamin asked one day.

"I don't think Reuben hates me."

Reuben was the eldest of the family.

"Well, perhaps *he* likes you a little," agreed Benjamin, "but all the others hate you. You know they do. Why?"

"Well, for one
thing, they don't
like father giving
me presents,"
said Joseph, "but
I don't think that's
the real reason."

"No?"

"No. I'm afraid
they think our father
will leave everything
to me when he dies
and they'll get nothing."

"Would he do that?"
Joseph shook his head.
"It doesn't seem likely.
Anyway, I don't think
I'll always be living here.
I've had such strange
dreams lately."

"What sort of dreams?"

But it didn't seem as if Joseph could tell just what they were yet. Perhaps he couldn't remember those first dreams. As time went by, he found he had a dream almost every night. And the strange thing was that although each dream was about something different, each one seemed to have the same meaning.

It was harvest time when the family first heard about them. Everyone was helping in the fields. All day long, the men and women, boys and girls of Jacob's big family worked together.

Some cut down the golden grain. Some tied it in bundles, called sheaves. Some loaded the sheaves on the back of donkeys to be carried to where other men were stacking them.

Everywhere there was talk and laughter as the family enjoyed their day in the open. Everywhere that is, except where Joseph worked. As soon as he came near one of his brothers, they made spiteful remarks.

"Look out, can't you see where you're going?" Levi said, pushing him roughly.

"Can't you do *anything* right?" snapped Judah. "That isn't the way to tie a sheaf."

"Where's your wonderful coat?" jeered Dan. "I thought you wore it *always*."

Joseph tried to avoid them as far as possible and he was glad when the day was over. He lay down beside Benjamin on their sleeping mat.

"That was a hard day's work," he said. "We'll be able to sleep without rocking tonight."

"I'm tired, too," said Benjamin, who had spent the time running after Joseph and trying to help.

"Of course you are," Joseph said, giving him a hug. "Now curl up and go to sleep."

   But Benjamin found it
hard, because his big
brother was so restless.
Joseph tossed and turned and
muttered to himself.

   "I suppose he's having one of those
dreams again," Benjamin thought.

   Next morning when the family
gathered for breakfast, Joseph said, "I
had a dream last night."

Benjamin nodded wisely.
"I thought so," he said to himself.

He felt quite
excited because he
saw that Joseph had
remembered this
dream. Joseph raised
his voice so that every-
one could hear,
"Last night I had a strange
dream."

They all stopped eating and
listened to him. People in
those days thought dreams had
a special meaning. And it was true
that God sometimes had used dreams
to guide men. Joseph went on,

"I dreamt that we were out in the
harvest fields again. We were tying
the grain into sheaves. Each of
the family had one sheaf. Sud-
denly, all the other sheaves
stood on end. Then they
bowed to my sheaf."

There was silence for a minute while the others thought about what Joseph had said. Then they all spoke at once,

"Do you mean to say you're better than we are?"

"You *must* be dreaming if you think I'd bow down to *you*."

"Are you crazy? Imagine me doing a thing like that!"

In the midst of all the noise, Benjamin slipped his hand into Joseph's.

"*I* wouldn't mind bowing to him," he thought. "I wouldn't mind at all."

Joseph knew his other brothers would dislike him more than ever, if that were possible. Yet somehow he just couldn't help telling them about his dream.

Soon the same thing happened again. This time, he could see the night sky through the opening in the tent. In his dream, he seemed to be part of that sky and that the rest of his family were there with him. Next day, he reported his dream.

"I thought I was a star. It was strange, because both the sun and the moon were in the sky at the same time. I felt that you were the sun, father, and my step-mother was the moon. Each of you, my brothers, was also a star — eleven of them, all shining brightly. Then the sun and the moon and the eleven other stars stood on end and bowed to my star."

The same idea again. Even Jacob was cross with his favourite this time.

"Don't be so silly, Joseph," he said. "Fathers don't bow to their sons."

The other brothers were really furious.

"He must think he's going to be a king," they muttered. "We'll show him!"

From that time they whispered

together whenever they saw him. They gave him a nickname —"The Dreamer." Often they wondered how they could get rid of him, and the time came when they even had the terrible thought of killing him. Finally, they had the chance of selling him as a slave and that's just what they did.

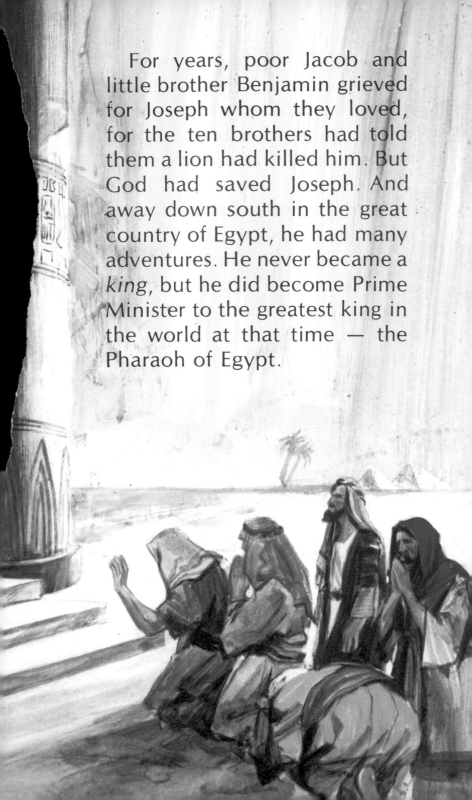

For years, poor Jacob and little brother Benjamin grieved for Joseph whom they loved, for the ten brothers had told them a lion had killed him. But God had saved Joseph. And away down south in the great country of Egypt, he had many adventures. He never became a *king*, but he did become Prime Minister to the greatest king in the world at that time — the Pharaoh of Egypt.

Twenty years passed before Joseph's dreams came true, but one day they did. His brothers visited Egypt asking the great Prime Minister of Egypt to give them food, because there was a terrible drought in their own country. They bowed low to him, because he was such an important man. Joseph knew *them*, although they didn't dream he was their brother. Instead of paying them back for the way they had treated him, Joseph was kind and helped them all he could.

And, on the day he told them who he really was, it was to Benjamin he turned first. Benjamin was the brother he still loved and remembered, although neither of them were boys any more.

Joseph's dreams of greatness came true. People everywhere heard of the wise and good Prime Minister of Egypt and asked his advice. But Joseph showed how great he really was, by helping those who had treated him so badly and repaying hate with kindness.